VOCAL SELECTION

CALL ME MADAM

Lyrics and Music by
IRVING BERLIN

Contents

Irving Berlin Music·Company®

EXCLUSIVELY DISTRIBUTED BY

Hal•Leonard CORPORATION

7777 W. BLUEMOUND RD. P.O. BOX 13819 MILWAUKEE, WI 53213

© Copyright 1965 by Irving Berlin
International Copyright Secured   All Rights Reserved

The Hostess With The Mostes' On The Ball

Tune Ukelele

A D F# B

Words and Music by
IRVING BERLIN

© Copyright 1950 by Irving Berlin
© Copyright Renewed
International Copyright Secured   All Rights Reserved

4

Chorus
Medium Jump Tempo

I'm the cho - sen par - ty giv - er for the
tain - ing vod - ka drink - ers is a

White House cli - en - tele ____ And they know that I de - liv -
job they give to me ____ Mak - ing nice guys out of stink-

- er What it takes to make 'em jell ____ And in
- ers Seems to be my cup of tea ____ What they

Wash - ing - ton I'm known by one and all _____ As the
real - ly need be - hind ____ the i - ron wall _____ Is the

HOS-TESS WITH THE MOS-TES' ON THE BALL _____ They would
There's a

go to El - sa Max - well When they had an ax to grind_ They could
book of reg - u - la - tions As to who sits next to who_ But there

al - ways grind their ax well At the par - ties she de - signed_ But the
may be com - pli - ca - tions When the blue blood's not so blue_ So the

hat-chet grind-ers now pre - fer to call _____ On the
priest-ess with the least - es' pro - to - col _____ Is the

Marrying For Love

Tune Ukelele

A D F# B

Words and Music by
IRVING BERLIN

© Copyright 1950 by Irving Berlin
© Copyright Renewed
International Copyright Secured   All Rights Reserved

Something To Dance About

Tune Ukulele

A D F# B

Words and Music by
IRVING BERLIN

Verse:
An old hand at giv-ing par-ties And I've learned an
aw-ful lot ___ The best rea-son for a par-ty
And what keeps it boil-ing hot ___ an oc-ca-sion when you've got ___

© Copyright 1950 by Irving Berlin
© Copyright Renewed
International Copyright Secured   All Rights Reserved

Chorus

SOME-THING TO DANCE A-BOUT___ Some-one to dance it with___

Some-thing to dance it to___ To a fox-trot___ or a waltz.___

Put on your danc-ing shoes___ Here comes some hap-py news___

Break up in twos and twos___ To a fox-trot or a waltz.___

You and some-one have part-ed___ And your lone-ly heart yearns

Once Upon A Time, Today

Words and Music by
IRVING BERLIN

© Copyright 1950 by Irving Berlin
© Copyright Renewed
International Copyright Secured · All Rights Reserved

(I Wonder Why?)

You're Just In Love

Tune Ukelele
A D F# B

Words and Music by
IRVING BERLIN

Moderato

1st Chorus

dreamily

I hear sing-ing and there's no one there ___ I smell

blos-soms and the trees are bare ___ All day long I seem to

walk on air, ___ I won-der why? ___ I won-der why? ___

© Copyright 1950 by Irving Berlin
© Copyright Renewed
International Copyright Secured   All Rights Reserved

(Dance To The Music Of)

The Ocarina

Tune Ukelele

A D F♯ B

Words and Music by
IRVING BERLIN

© Copyright 1950 by Irving Berlin
© Copyright Renewed
International Copyright Secured   All Rights Reserved

Dance to the mu-sic of THE OC-A-RI-NA, OC - A - RI-NA, OC - A-RI-NA,

Gret-chen and Ot-to, Hans and Wil - hel-mi-na Dance to THE OC-A-RI-NA dance.

Dance to the mu-sic of the sweet po-ta-ta, sweet po-ta-ta, sweet po-ta-ta

Cheeks get-tin' red-der than a ripe to-ma-ta Dance to THE OC-A-RI-NA dance

Lis-ten and hear the notes es-cap-ing Out of that ti - ny hole

Does-n' it please your soul Does-n' it say "Dance the pol - ka"

Step to the mu-sic of THE OC - A - RI - NA Who re-fus-es? Wil - hel-mi - na?

Wait till she lis-tens to THE OC - A - RI - NA I know that Wil-hel-mi-na will. will.

It's A Lovely Day Today

Tune Ukelele

A D F♯ B

Words and Music by
IRVING BERLIN

IT'S A LOVE-LY DAY TO-DAY__ So what-ev-er you've got to do __ You've got a

love-ly day to do it in that's true _____ And I hope what-ev-er you've

got to do is some-thing that can be done by two For I'd real-ly

© Copyright 1950 by Irving Berlin
© Copyright Renewed
International Copyright Secured   All Rights Reserved

Washington Square Dance

Tune Ukelele

A   D   F#   B

Words and Music by
IRVING BERLIN

Square dance ___ The WASHNG-TON SQUARE DANCE ___ Re-pub-li-cans

make up with the Dem-o-crats Show those for-eign dip-lo-mats that you

© Copyright 1950 by Irving Berlin
© Copyright Renewed
International Copyright Secured   All Rights Reserved

Show our friends a - cross the sea It's a fair
square dance _____ The WASH-ING-TON
dance _____ The WASH-ING-TON

SQUARE DANCE _____ The rules are the same as crick - et, golf or squash
SQUARE DANCE _____ Be care - ful you'll have to watch your step, by gosh _

No fair cheat - ing 'cause the WASH-ING-TON SQUARE DANCE _____ is
No roundheels be - cause the WASH-ING-TON SQUARE DANCE _____ is

To Patter

Fine

square. _____ square. _____

Patter

Bow to your part - ners ____ Bow to your cor - ners ____

Dance till your cheeks are red as a rose But try not to step on Mc - Car - ty's toes Now

duck for the oy - ster ____ Dig for the clam ____

Duck for the oy - ster, dig for the clam But do your dig-ging for Un - cle Sam— And

one for the mon-ey_____ Two for the show _____

One for the mon-ey, Two for the show and three to get read-y for Un-cle Joe. Re-

pub-li-cans o-ver to the right. ___ Dem-o-crats o-ver to the left. _____ The

left meet the right and don't ex-plode Try to find the mid-dle of the road and

D.S. al Fine

The Best Thing For You

Tune Ukelele

A D F♯ B

Words and Music by
IRVING BERLIN

Verse (ad lib.)

Please let me say from the start I don't pre-tend to be smart.

I just sug-gest, what I think best, Hav-ing your in-t'rest at heart.

© Copyright 1950 by Irving Berlin
© Copyright Renewed
International Copyright Secured   All Rights Reserved